The Common Sense Guide to Publicity

**Practical advice on how to
use the power of publicity
to enhance image and perception,
create awareness and
promote products and services**

John DeFrancesco and Gary Goodfriend

DeFrancesco/Goodfriend Public Relations
444 North Michigan Avenue, Suite 1000, Chicago, IL 60611

THE COMMON SENSE GUIDE TO PUBLICITY

For information about permission to reproduce selections
from this book, write to the authors at
DeFrancesco/Goodfriend Public Relations
444 N. Michigan Avenue
Suite 1000
Chicago, IL 60611

Phone: 312-644-4409
Fax: 312-644-7651
e-mail: office@dgpr.com

ISBN: 0-9650398-0-3

PRINTED IN THE UNITED STATES OF AMERICA

10 9 8 7 6 5 4 3 2

This book is dedicated to

Mitzi Nowakowski,

a co-founder and partner
of DeFrancesco/Goodfriend and our friend,
whose talent, dedication and encouragement
have contributed immensely
to the company's success.

CONTENTS

PART THREE:
TACTICS THAT GUARANTEE
A SUCCESSFUL PUBLICITY PROGRAM

PART FOUR:
CASE HISTORIES --
IDEAS YOU CAN USE

PREFACE

Many good books on publicity already have been published. So why write another?

Our aim is to offer you *practical information*. We've cut through clutter and theory to provide a handy reference for working with the media to gain publicity.

What makes this book different is its quick-reading and quick-reference style. You won't have to wade through dozens of pages to glean key points for dealing with the media, and you can refer to any chapter as a reminder, if needed.

We're sharing with you our insider tips based on a combined total of nearly 60 years of experience in "working the media" to gain publicity for hundreds of clients in dozens of industries.

You'll find this guide useful if you are:

- A *business owner or manager* who wants a better understanding of publicity as a marketing and image-building vehicle.

- A *public relations practitioner* who wants a reference on workable techniques.

- A *student or recent graduate* entering the public relations profession.

- A *volunteer* who is charged with gaining publicity exposure for an organization.

- ◆ A *trade association executive* who wants to educate members on self-promotion.

- ◆ A *person* curious to know more about how things get publicized.

Much of the material in this book was adapted from workshops we have conducted throughout the United States for business executives, as well as for college students. We know the techniques work...we trust they will benefit you.

Part One

Put the Power of Publicity to Work for You

Demystifying the Myths of Publicity

Publicity. It's the foundation for nearly every company's public relations program. Positive publicity exposure on a consistent basis can benefit a company's image, enhance perception on the part of its key audiences and help market the firm's products or services.

Yet, many myths and misconceptions exist regarding how and why press coverage is generated. Here are the most common fallacies:

♦   **In publicity, it's not what you know, it's who you know.** If a company doesn't have a strong, timely story to tell to the media, it doesn't matter what editorial contacts you have. Editors first consider the "reader value" of a story idea: Will this story be meaningful and of interest to the publication's audience? Therefore, even if the editor is a long-time friend, he or she won't use the information unless it's newsworthy.

♦   **If my company places an ad in a magazine, then we deserve to receive editorial coverage.** True, a few trade publications admit a direct relationship between advertising and editorial coverage. However, the majority of media keep editorial and advertising separate and distinct. Also, many editors take offense when it is suggested that their publications "should" provide favorable coverage because an ad has been purchased.

♦ **Small editorial mentions don't really make much of an impact**. While a cover story profiling a company is of great editorial value, companies shouldn't overlook the benefits of smaller editorial mentions. For example, a brief story on a product that is new or has an unusual application can generate inquiries for more information.

♦ **Publicity will work only if my company has a big story to tell**. Companies that subscribe to this philosophy are missing important publicity opportunities. An effective means of garnering editorial coverage is announcing "news" such as a relocation or expansion, open houses, new personnel, staff promotions, company anniversaries, awards and other developments or milestones.

♦ **We sent out a press release last week. Why haven't we seen any coverage yet?** Possibly the most misunderstood aspect of publicity is the lead time required for different types of publications. Unless a press release involves "hard" immediate news, it may not appear for weeks or months. Consumer and trade magazines may have lead times of three or four months. Many publications work from an annual editorial calendar that maps out the topics to be covered in each edition. As a result, an editor may hold the release for use in the most appropriate issue. Or, the editor may use the article as part of an overview or in a round-up story.

♦ **Our story appeared on the cover of a key publication. Why haven't sales increased yet?** Another aspect of publicity that is difficult to accept is that publicity, in most cases, is not a direct sales-building vehicle. Publicity will increase awareness of a company's products, services or people, improve its reputation and convey a positive image.

Such benefits also will condition target audiences to be more receptive to a sales call...and ultimately contribute to the bottom line.

Merchandise Publicity to Extend Reach

If positive newspaper and magazine articles are simply placed in a drawer or file, you could be filing away one of your most valuable marketing tools.

By merchandising reprints of articles, companies can extend the publicity message far beyond its original readership. When sent to the appropriate target audience, such as customers and prospects, favorable stories can provide an objective, third-party endorsement of a firm's products or services, demonstrate a leadership position and foster confidence in your company.

Reprints can be used in direct mail, as leave-behinds in meetings and as part of sales presentations. Presented in this manner, the reprints often can yield rewards more valuable than publicity alone.

To make the most of your media mentions, follow these guidelines:

♦ Don't assume everyone has read the original article. A front-page mention in a major metropolitan paper doesn't guarantee that your best customers have read it. To ensure an article reaches your intended audience, take the direct route -- send it yourself, with an appropriate cover note.

- ◆ Circulate the article internally. Distribute copies to employees to show how the media perceive the firm.

- ◆ Display the article. Frame the article for display on a wall or tabletop, place copies on the table in your reception area, or create a company "publicity scrap book" so guests may read the articles.

- ◆ Use excerpts. Publish portions of the article in a company newsletter or sales brochure. Be sure to include the name of the publication in which the story appeared.

- ◆ Use reprints to get more coverage. When attempting to obtain additional media coverage, send copies of the reprints to non-competing media as credible background material. For example, a newspaper article can be sent to trade publications.

- ◆ Use the story as part of a high-impact presentation. A company featured in a local newspaper article had the story reproduced on ceramic coffee mugs that were presented to prospects during sales calls.

By utilizing methods to maximize your publicity, your "first impression" doesn't have to be your last.

The Media Universe

Daily newspapers are dying, talk shows essentially focus on the bizarre...and it seems everyone is seeking information through the Internet.

Are there enough media outlets available today to disseminate your organization's messages?

Absolutely. The media universe remains vast. You just need to know that opportunities for publicity go well beyond the business page and TV news coverage:

♦ **Trade Magazines**. There is a trade journal for just about any industry, any product, any service in America. How about these titles: *Play Meter*, for the coin-operated amusement industry; *Rock Products*, for those in nonmetallic mining; *The Cheese Reporter*, read by cheese producers; and *VAR Business*, for value-added resellers and dealers of computer products. Don't overlook these publications! In addition to product information, many will publish articles under your byline on topics relevant to their readers. Such stories make great reprints.

♦ **Regional Business Journals**. Nearly every state, region and major city are "home" to a magazine or newspaper that covers local business news.

However, many editors will use materials from sources based anywhere in the country if they believe the information will benefit readers. A national accounts receivable management firm based in Chicago continually provides cash flow advice for readers of journals in Ohio, North Carolina, San Diego, Savannah, Sacramento, Minneapolis and many others.

♦ **National Business Magazines**. Yes, a profile in *Forbes* or *Fortune* is a coup, but extremely difficult to secure. So, don't neglect journals that you may think have less "stature," yet are quite influential with many readers, such as *Nation's Business*, *Independent Business* and *Entrepreneur*. Identify highly read columns in all of these journals that are more likely to use information from public relations people (examples: "Business Bulletin" in *The Wall Street Journal*, "Economic Trends" in *Business Week*).

♦ **Consumer Magazines**. Here, too, check out regular columns in the national publications, identify the increasing number of regional journals (examples: *Midwest Living*, *Chicago Parent*) and learn about new titles unveiled every year, usually very audience or topic specific (examples: *Outside Kids*, *Fine Cooking*).

♦ **News Wires/Syndicated Columns**. Want to gain coverage in multiple newspapers with just one placement of a news release? Consider a news wire such as *Associated Press* or one of the hundreds of columns that are syndicated to papers nationwide. The latter can be especially fertile because of their numbers and focus. Do you market a product sold in hardware stores? Consider columns such as "Super Handyman" or "Home Workshop File." Are you an expert on personal finance issues? Try contacting "Bondy on Money" or "Personal Finance." One enterprising firm gained coverage by placing an historical fact in the "Ripley's Believe It Or Not" syndicated cartoon panel.

♦ **Newspapers**. The best approach here: Figuratively tear the paper apart and identify the paper's various sections, columns and features that offer avenues for coverage. You may discover "new" options...such as a "city digest" column or the "letters to the editor" section.

♦ **Television**. Of course, today you have the local news shows, with more scheduled in morning, noon and late afternoon time slots (in addition to evening). Network news and national talk shows are other obvious targets. But also approach national and local news magazines, local "issues oriented" programs, the numerous cable network programs that focus on specific topics (such as travel, food, fashion) and the growing number of syndicated programs, many which replicate the "how to" consumer magazines. Creative, timely approaches can net coverage you may only dream about. One kitchen appliance company sent an unusual product it made to Andy Rooney...in case he was planning a special segment on unique Christmas gifts. Andy showed -- and used -- the product on such a "60 Minutes" segment, seen by millions.

♦ **Radio**. Here, too, go beyond the obvious. Networks exist that focus solely on business, such as *The Wall Street Journal Radio Network* and *Business News Network*. The proliferation of sports talk stations may offer opportunities; companies involved with promotions or products that involve sports could gain coverage. Local stations may regularly run segments on issues such as health, food and the environment that may prove invaluable for gaining air time.

Part Two

How to Work With the Media

4

How to Build a Media Contact List

It sounds mundane, tedious and humdrum. The deed does not immediately place you in the publicity spotlight.

But, development of a thorough, well-thought-out list of media you wish to target is the first and crucial step in beginning a publicity program.

Yet, before you start, it's essential not to get "caught up" in the excitement and target media outlets that don't make sense.

Really, why be on "Oprah," as glamorous as that sounds, if you market a product used in metalworking plants, even if the item is the only one of its kind? Would not a cover photo in *Metalworking Digest* better influence potential buyers?

Or, say you need to increase consumer sales of your new cookie product. An item in *The Wall Street Journal* may be great for the ego, but a story sent to newspaper food editors via the national *Associated Press* news wire can more precisely reach the country's cookie monsters (and shoppers).

To begin, you must determine which media are read, viewed and listened to by your target audiences. Hopefully, you already have a clear understanding of just whom your target audiences are. (If not, save reading this book for another time; you need to get your marketing plan in order first.)

To illustrate: Skil Power Tools markets a number of its products to woodworkers and consumers who tackle do-it-yourself jobs and projects around the house. The target media for Skil, in this case, are magazines such as *Popular Mechanics, Workbench, Home Mechanix, The Family Handyman* and *Wood*; national newspaper columns titled "Super Handyman" and "Home Workshop File"; home sections of daily newspapers; and the trade journals read by the retailers who sell Skil tools to these end-users, such as *Hardware Age* and *National Home Center News*.

For Tarcom Corporation, a Chicago-area general contractor who specializes in office interiors and build-outs, the focus is not consumer publicity. Instead, it's publicity in publications read by business people, real estate executives and those Tarcom has identified as key markets -- in health care, legal and retailing. Local publicity is more relevant in Tarcom's case, although coverage in a targeted national journal will still reach a number of readers based in Chicago. So, the target list includes *Metro Chicago Real Estate, Chicago Industrial Properties, Chicago Tribune, Illinois Legal Times, Hospital Trustee* and others.

Okay, you've identified the audiences; how do you develop this media list? There are several techniques:

♦ **Use media directories**. A number of directories are available that offer listings and descriptions of nearly every media outlet in existence. Bacon's Directories, for example, provide thorough listings of consumer and trade magazines, newspapers, and radio and television stations and programs. In major markets, some local organizations offer directories in their respective cities. The Publicity Club of Chicago, for instance, has an excellent directory that covers the greater Chicago metro area and Illinois.

♦ **Get to know media you believe would reach your target audience**. Familiarize yourself with bylines, columns and special sections. If you're in real estate, know who the real estate editor and/or reporter is

14

for the local newspaper. If you seek a story about an innovative marketing technique your company offers, and coverage in *Inc.* magazine would reach your audience, you should know that the magazine has a special column on marketing called "Hands On, Sales & Marketing." Plus, learn the name of the editor of the column.

♦ **Call a media outlet directly to pinpoint its editorial focus**. Ask who would be the appropriate person to receive your press materials and can be contacted. Media people appreciate companies that take the time to identify names of reporters and the news beats they cover. And, always be sure to spell their names accurately.

♦ **Update lists periodically**. There's a high turnover rate in the media. So, you will need to update your target list periodically. This is accomplished by always reviewing bylines, maintaining personal contact and, if directories are used, receiving updates from those companies.

♦ **Purchase media lists**. One last option is to purchase a media list much like you would buy a mailing list for a direct mail program. Two companies that provide this service are Bacon's and Associated Release Service.

5

Throw Your Best Pitch
to Pique Media Attention

With those media targets now in place, it's time to contact the editors, reporters and broadcasters.

And, unless your story is what we call hard news that requires immediate attention (this is usually negative, like a fire, strike or accident; or, perhaps, some dignitary visits your company on the spur of the moment), it's not necessary nor usually desirable to call the media contacts first.

Plus, for starters, you may not need to laboriously write a press release. Instead, often the best approach is to write a letter -- a query, or "pitch," letter -- that outlines your suggestion for a story on some aspect of your company.

Now, if you've become familiar with the media you're contacting, you should know a story won't appear just because you're a nice person, the company makes money and people love your product or service.

No, you have to develop an angle that makes your story idea different, interesting, meaningful, trendy or a host of other adjectives. You must explain why the newspaper, magazine or broadcaster should devote valuable space or airtime to your story. Some elements that will help your story be newsworthy:

> ♦ **Make it timely**. Tie your idea to a recent trend or news angle of relevance to the readers, listeners or viewers. Such a lead might read, "The current surge

in mortgage refinancing has boosted sales for one Texas company that manufactures mortgage slide calculators."

♦ **Make it seasonal**. Annually, opportunities exist to gain coverage linked to a certain season or holiday. To illustrate:

♦♦ "This year is expected to be a boom year for holiday spending, but many consumers may go bust." (For a collection agency).

♦♦ "October 3 begins National Fire Prevention Week...smoke alarms have helped reduce fire deaths by 50 percent. The key with smoke detectors is they must be installed and maintained properly." (For a smoke alarm manufacturer).

♦ **Tie it to some natural news at your company**. This could be a new product introduction; an anniversary; an office relocation, expansion or groundbreaking; a human interest angle; or a company milestone, such as a sales or production record. One such lead, used successfully by a marketer of a new potassium chloride water softener product: "For the many Indiana households that use water softening systems, the health benefits of potassium are now available simply by turning on the faucet."

Here are some tips for writing the all-important pitch letter:

♦ **Be brief**. Try to limit the letter to one page. Media receive dozens of these letters a day and their reading time is at a premium. Create eye appeal for your letter by writing concise sentences and short paragraphs; use bullet points to enhance readability.

♦ **Write the "lead" of the story to start the letter**. Many effective pitch letters often provide the right framework for the story that you hope will be written ultimately, or the TV segment that will be produced eventually. By doing this, you're graphically showing the editor how your idea comes to life.

Following are two actual uses:

♦♦ "If you thought your mother's dining room table was too fancy to eat on, wait until you see a local artist's latest furniture creations." (For a local retailer).

♦♦ "What motivates a company to build a $7 million Medieval castle in what likely was once a Midwest cornfield in a Chicago suburb?" (For a unique dinner/theater facility).

♦ **Provoke the reader**. One way to accomplish this is to begin a pitch letter with a question or a startling statistic:

♦♦ "Every June, thousands of couples tie the knot and marry. But June isn't a happy month for all couples -- according to the Census Bureau, it's also the month when the most number of divorces become final." (For a financial planner).

♦♦   "Some 75,000,000 bicyclists in this country greatly endanger themselves every time they pedal their two-wheelers. How? By not using their heads...and protecting them. (For a bike helmet manufacturer.)

♦ **Don't oversell or make your letter sound like a commercial**. Remember, you're not trying to run an advertisement. The letter must spell out why the story or segment will benefit the media outlet's audience.

♦ **Know what the reporter has been covering and tie your idea to it**. Investigate what the target media person has been reporting recently and reflect this knowledge in your pitch letter. You will appear "involved" in the journalist's activities. Even if he declines your pitch this time, he may be more amenable on your next effort.

♦ **Send background materials, if appropriate**. A company brochure, a news release, a photo or even an article published in a non-competing media outlet (e.g., a trade magazine story if pitching a newspaper) may be enclosed with the letter to provide additional background.

♦ **Plan to follow up**. Close the letter. State you will follow up by telephone within the next few days to discuss the story idea with the editor/producer.

Making the Media Follow-Up Call

You've mailed the pitch letter; now it's time to make the follow-up call.

One word of warning: Some media people don't like to receive follow-up calls. The reasons are two-fold.

First, the volume of such calls they receive daily can be heavy; second, far too many of these calls simply ask the questions "Did you receive my press release?" and "When will you use my press release?"

Such calls should *never* be made. They indeed are major nuisances for media people and will damage your relationships with your media contacts.

However, since your pitch letter was individualized for a specific editor and proposed a story idea, a follow-up call is more acceptable. Some guidelines:

- ◆ After introducing yourself, start by asking "Are you on deadline?" or "Is this a good time for you to talk for a few moments?" This shows you know and respect the pressures faced by media.

- ◆ Mention the letter and discuss the merits of the story idea and gauge the interest of the editor or producer.

- ◆ Don't be surprised that editors claim they never saw the letter or background. This happens frequently, often due to the volume of mail they receive or an initial review they do not recall. Therefore, it may be necessary for you to make the pitch from the start without the benefit of the editor having any background. Be prepared for this.

♦ Other times, editors will ask that you resend the materials. In such cases, write on the envelope "As Requested"; this should prompt greater attention from the recipient.

♦ You also may run into the latest curse among public relations practitioners -- voice mail. You'll just have to be persistent with your messages. If your call is never returned, you'll just have to assume that this particular media person did not find your idea of immediate interest.

♦ If at first you don't succeed, don't give up. Perhaps you should try a different media contact at the same outlet. Or, try again in a couple of months with a different angle...or even a variation of the first angle. Sometimes, timing is everything.

Through this process, you'll also learn how specific media people prefer to be "pitched." Many appreciate the letter and follow-up call. Others will review the letter, but will tell you if they're interested, they'll call you back; don't bother to follow up. (Although most practitioners still hope to make a voice contact in case the information was not received or given just a cursory look.)

Some may favor a one-page fax, while others demand that the fax only be used if they request it.

One secret to all of this is to develop working relationships that are mutually beneficial.

How to Establish Yourself as a Source for Media

One of the ways you can position yourself to be quoted in the media is to take advantage of opportunities presented by the current events reported daily by the press.

Media look to experts in various fields who can provide authoritative commentary or analysis. Plus, media on all levels are more issue-oriented. TV and radio talk shows seek guests who can take knowledgeable positions on current issues to generate audience reaction and response.

Many companies have capitalized on these media needs to gain exposure. For example:

♦ The National Energy Policy Act bans use of certain popular yet non-energy efficient commercial lights, forcing thousands of companies to replace lighting systems. When the policy was announced, an electrical contracting firm wrote an article for a trade journal on the effect of the legislation and the lighting alternatives for industrial facilities. The article positioned the firm as a knowledgeable source among its buyer-audiences.

♦ Government and industry reports and forecasts also provide opportunities. An outplacement services company that tracks national job market trends prepared remarks on the monthly unemployment statistics issued by the U.S. Labor Department. It offered this commitment to *Associated Press* each month when the news service was preparing its round-up story on unemployment.

♦ During a period of tight credit, a news release was developed quoting the president of a commercial collections firm on unusual debtor excuses. The story was published by a newspaper and, in turn, the individual was called to be interviewed for a national TV news segment.

♦ Speculation over the direction of interest rates provided a bank the opportunity to have its economist offer views on where rates were headed.

Following are some ways you can establish yourself or your associates as a source for media:

♦ Identify the most important media covering your field. Make a list of the reporters and writers; find out who the editors are. Include all-news radio stations and radio and TV stations that broadcast talk shows.

♦ Send to media information on your company, a list of the expertise of individuals at your firm and the topics they can address. Include a rolodex card or an index file card listing your company's name, address, areas of expertise and the names and phone numbers of the contact sources.

♦ Offer to meet with the editors or reporters who cover topics on which you can comment in order to get acquainted. Media people are more likely to contact individuals they know and feel comfortable with as a source.

- ♦ Keep abreast of current events. Read at least two daily newspapers and your local business journal in addition to the TV or radio news shows you may watch or listen to.

- ♦ Call the media in reaction to a "breaking" story, but only when you have something meaningful to offer.

- ♦ Return all media calls promptly. Reporters and writers observe tight deadlines and the degree of your responsiveness often will dictate whether you are included in the story.

When you read something negative in the paper about, or that may affect, your industry, it may make you "see red." But, you also can view it as a chance to tell a positive story through a letter to the editor of the publication. Here are some tips for drafting a letter to the editor:

- ♦ Don't blow your cool or be antagonistic. Your letter may get into print, but you probably won't like the result. Some editors are perverse enough to publish emotional but inarticulate protests.

- ♦ Keep your letter brief, to one page if possible. Long letters may be edited, possibly to your disadvantage.

- ♦ Humor or *mild* sarcasm can be effective and can add to reader interest. Just don't overdo it.

- ♦ Call attention to contradictions and flaws in the story. Quote facts and statistics when you can.

♦ Before you mail your letter, have another person read the letter who can be counted on to give a candid opinion.

By taking pro-active measures to comment in the press on current events, you can enhance the awareness and image of your company.

8

How to Survive Media Interviews

An interview with the press often can leave even the most outspoken executive at a loss for words. Yet, media interviews provide an extremely effective way for companies to communicate to the audiences they want to reach.

Proper preparation, therefore, is essential to ensure that the interview meets your goals and those of the reporter. Here are several tips to help your interview run more smoothly.

Before the interview:

♦ Prepare a list of key messages you wish to make.

♦ Prepare "evidence" -- facts that prove your messages and make them credible.

♦ Think of tough topics or sensitive questions you may be asked and formulate answers that include your key messages.

♦ Know the type of audience that reads the publication or tunes into the program and tailor your messages for it.

- Translate your messages to include the phrase, "...and what this means to your audience..."

During the interview:

- Take the initiative; be prepared to give information; answer a question and go on with the kinds of comments you've practiced.

- Be honest, never hedge and never, never lie to the press.

- Be personal, not too stiff, too smooth or overbearing.

- Use positive words and phrases when you answer questions.

- Be aware of body language. Look the reporter in the eye; don't swing your legs around or slump in your chair.

- Assume that everything you say can be used as a quote.

- Be energetic. An expressive face, a well-modulated, lively voice and appropriate gestures will help maintain the interviewer's interest.

After the interview:

- Offer your schedule and phone number to the reporter in case he/she has further questions.

♦   Always be gracious, even if the interview was challenging or even non-productive.

Thorough preparation and planning can help you feel more at ease and result in more productive interviews for both your company and the media.

9

Everything You Say Can be Used (Sometimes Against You)

"Off-the-record" and "don't quote me" are clichés that have been used frequently in fictionalized accounts of dialog between a reporter and interviewee (or "information source"). In the movies, those phrases usually protect the source from being quoted.

Real life can be, and frequently is, different. When being interviewed, giving information off-the-record can be dangerous if you really don't want to have the information published.

The best policy is *never* say anything to a reporter that you wouldn't want to see in print or used in a broadcast. Why should you? There is no reason to give a reporter more information than necessary for the story. Letting the reporter in on insider information, trade secrets, assumptions or personal opinion related to your company is unnecessary. Apply the old military policy regarding transfer of information, "need to know." If they don't need to know it, don't tell it to them.

Even if the reporter agrees to keep your anonymity, he or she may use the information and attribute the quote to a "company spokesperson." People can usually deduce the real source. That could prove embarrassing.

When asked a question, either answer it or tell the reporter you can't answer it, but never think you're safe responding within an off-the-record context.

10

How to Build Favorable Relationships With Media

Relationships between business and the news media sometimes are marked by acrimony and misunderstanding, but it need not be that way.

Favorable media relations are important to business in gaining the desired visibility before targeted audiences and communicating the story it wants to be told.

Following are ways you can foster better media relations:

♦ Build bridges. Deal candidly and truthfully with reporters. If there are questions that you cannot answer for reasons of policy, acknowledge that fact rather than mislead the media.

♦ Tour your local newspapers and TV stations. Meet with the appropriate editors to find out how newsrooms operate.

♦ Seek out editors, reporters and assignment editors who someday may have a reason to cover or assign coverage of your company. If you have any complaints and/or suggestions, you are much more likely to be heard if you are known to the media.

- Always ask for correction of an error. For a damaging error, seek prominent placement of the correction. But you can't expect prominent correction of a relatively minor error.

- If you feel a reporter is consistently unfair, you are well within your rights to complain to the editor or publisher.

- Realize that reporters' standards require them to remain detached and not become either friends or enemies.

- Keep the long-term reputation of the company in mind through every action. Listen as closely to a qualified public relations counselor as you would a lawyer or financial officer.

- Remember that reporters are not merely transcribers. More than ever before, they are being asked to analyze, not just report.

- Be open and honest. Do not expect your press release to appear exactly as your public relations counsel wrote it. The release is written to promote the company; the reporter is writing to inform the reader. Do not try to conceal bad news; the reporter will find it.

♦ Make communications a priority. Communicate equally well with your employees and the public. Remember that the media are part of the public. Make sure the top company official is the one the public sees and hears from the most often.

Applying these standards will enhance your company's relationships with editors.

11

Treat Media Deadlines With Respect

Everyone who has a job -- and even some who do not (e.g., students) -- faces deadlines.

Yet, the term deadline is likely linked closest to the editorial media world that includes the daily newspaper reporter, the TV news director and others (did you ever see that memorable scene from the movie *Broadcast News* to rush a segment on the air?).

To work best with the media, you need to know and understand the various deadlines each editorial outlet has established...and treat those deadlines with the utmost respect.

Obviously, deadlines differ based on the frequency of publishing or broadcast, "lead time" requirements and an outlet's own established procedures. To illustrate:

♦ Morning daily newspapers have daily deadlines, yet these vary. Regular columnists may have late afternoon deadlines; for sports and news pages, it can be late evening. Special sections (e.g., food, travel, Sunday sections) can have deadlines several days before publication date.

♦ Weekly newspapers often will have one or two days prior to publication deadline for news pages and sports sections. However, other sections (e.g., business, community events, etc.) could require that copy be turned in a week prior.

♦ Monthly national consumer magazines such as *Good Housekeeping*, *Better Homes & Gardens* and *Popular Mechanics* have, perhaps, the longest lead times...four to six months at times. Most of these publications work on their holiday issues in July.

♦ News wires such as *Associated Press* have deadlines that range from zero minutes (copy is transmitted immediately) to weeks. For example, the wire periodically distributes "Special Edition Packages" on a specific topic to its subscribers. However, AP needs lead time to prepare these sections. Deadline for its back-to-school package is late June; for winter travel, it's late September.

♦ Broadcast talk shows also have wide-ranging deadlines. Programs such as "Today" and "Larry King" can accommodate fast-breaking news events instantly. Yet, for less time-sensitive topics, such as author interviews or special product features, producers may prefer to be contacted a month in advance.

There's one other deadline we've not yet addressed: returning the call from the media person.

In such cases, whether it's a long-lead journal like *Woman's Day* or the daily *Chicago Tribune*, or whether it's a new products columnist or a business writer, only one deadline exists. Return the call now!

12

Check That Calendar for Publicity Pitches

Anticipating the editorial needs of magazines is one key to successful publicity programs. And, it's possible to garner this insight from editorial calendars available from publications.

Most trade, business and consumer magazines produce and distribute annual schedules of major topics planned for each issue. Depending on the publication, a calendar might indicate specific types of products that will be spotlighted in an issue, or general concepts and trends to be investigated.

For instance, you may find that this year's editorial calendar for *Hardware Age* indicates that power tools will be the focus in its May issue, while outdoor power equipment will be given special emphasis in July. The calendar for a different type of publication, *Nation's Business*, may list equipping the small office as a topic for its April issue and offers a guide to business software as its spotlight for the June issue.

Armed with this knowledge, you can provide materials to media at the most opportune times. To use this "inside" information most effectively, it is important to follow a few basic guidelines:

  ♦ **Check editorial deadlines**. Editorial calendars publish deadlines for advertisements, but do not always include closing dates for editorial material.

It is important to remember that editorial deadlines usually fall *before* those for advertising. It is well worth a phone call to the publication to check its editorial deadline.

- **Learn who is editing the issue or section**. If the name of the contact person is not included on the calendar, call the publication and learn who should receive the material. Send a personalized letter to that person clearly indicating how the provided information is appropriate for the issue.

- **Tailor material for the specific issue**. Present the editor with material in a manner so it will dove-tail with the issue and clarify why it is appropriate. Do not assume he or she will realize the connection. Provide suitable press releases and other background information. Position a company spokesperson as an expert and suggest arranging an interview.

- **Follow up by phone**. A week or so after the material is sent, contact the editor by phone. Again, emphasize how it is suitable for the target issue and offer to send additional information, if necessary. Gauge the magazine's interest and attempt to learn if, and how, the material will be used.

How do you obtain the valuable editorial calendar? Just call the publications. Most editors are pleased to provide it, or the magazine's advertising department will forward one to you as part of its media kit.

It is ideal to target media at a time when they are most receptive to an idea. An editorial calendar provides a great opportunity to be in the proverbial right place at the right time with a story idea.

13

Just Say 'No' to Press Conferences

Your boss thinks the company has the greatest new widget ever made and suggests a press conference to announce it to the world.

You send invitations to the media and call them. You start to perspire as one after another yawns at your pitch.

Worse, of the 25 media you've invited, only one person shows up at the conference -- an intern from *Widget Quarterly Gazette*.

You've just experienced one of the publicist's worst nightmares. And you still have to explain to the boss why you failed, even though the idea was a bummer from the start.

Face it, except in unusual cases, the traditional press conference concept has gone the way of the buggy whip. The media are short-staffed, too busy and they get too many invitations to possibly cover every event.

On any given day, in every major city, there are dozens of activities that may conflict with your planned conference. For every trade show, local and trade media are asked by most exhibitors to visit their booths. Many host expensive breakfast or luncheon events, only to discover that all their competitors have done the same thing. Reporters can't be in more than one place at a time.

Is there ever a time when a press conference is warranted? Yes, if:

♦ Your company is experiencing a crisis situation, such as the Tylenol, Exxon or Three-Mile Island disasters, a strike, an airline crash. Then you'll *need* to call the press together to explain your position.

♦ You have something truly revolutionary that makes the announcement newsworthy, such as a product with a new health benefit. But, don't decide the value based on subjective feelings; determine it objectively from the benefit to a reader of a publication. Check it with outside sources to get unbiased perceptions.

♦ You have some major findings to report based on research.

Of course, there are other situations that must be decided on a case by case basis. In general, however, just say "no" to press conferences.

You're much better off working one-on-one with media important to your company. Get to know them personally. Meet with them in their offices for briefings on new products or developments. Introduce editors/reporters to people within your company that can called upon as information sources.

14

Meet The Press --
at Their Desks

The term *desk top press conference* may conjure up visions of an executive addressing the media while standing on a desk, or perhaps some press event staged by an office furniture manufacturer.

Actually, it's a public relations term for a technique that can greatly enhance your editorial contacts and generate publicity.

Often utilized in lieu of a traditional press conference where many reporters assemble in a single location, the desk top variety involves a series of individual meetings with editors, reporters and producers in their offices -- across from their desks.

The purposes for the conferences can vary. Many companies use the tactic to introduce a new product or service. Others schedule the media meetings to explain a company's stance on an issue, review research findings or discuss placement opportunities.

The desk top press conference offers numerous benefits:

♦ Scheduling specific meetings ensures targeted media will receive and hear a company's message.

♦ The personal, one-to-one sessions help nurture media relationships.

♦ The format enables editors to more easily ask questions, not always possible in a public forum.

- Product demonstrations, in some cases, can be easier to implement.

One of the greatest advantages: The desk top approach provides greater scheduling flexibility for editors compared to the typical press conference. They do not need to leave their office nor be tied to one specific time to hear the presentation.

Many companies schedule desk top press conferences in New York because numerous major, national media are based there. The technique also is quite appropriate on a regional and local market basis.

Where to begin? As emphasized earlier in the chapters on what makes news and writing the pitch letter, you must have a "newsworthy" story to tell. Once that's in place:

- Develop your media target list.

- Identify who your media spokesperson will be. This may be an executive of the company, an outside expert (examples: a doctor, a professor, a celebrity or, yes, even a public relations representative).

- Contact the media by phone and/or letter and schedule the meetings. This should be done two to three weeks before the sessions will occur. You will find, however, based on editors' needs to remain flexible, that conferences will be scheduled right up to the day before.

- Suggest the meeting will take no longer than 15 minutes to help you literally get your foot in the door.

- Send confirmation letters to all.

♦ Prepare background information to leave with the media, whether in the form of a press kit, news releases, product brochures...or even product samples.

♦ Rehearse the spokesperson's presentation similarly to preparing for an interview.

15

How Promotional Products Can Enhance Relationships With Editors

Relationship-building. While it's the trend of the '90s in marketing communications to customers, building relationships with editors always has been a cornerstone of all productive publicity programs.

Today, technological advancements, ranging from the fax machine to the Internet and e-mail, are making it faster and more efficient to transmit information to the media. Conversely, technology may be contributing to an environment in which business and media people are losing personal contact with each other.

Compounding the problem are these facts:

♦ Editors have less time today; most media outlets operate with fewer editorial people and many editors and reporters are taking on more responsibilities. As a result, many won't take or return calls, preferring to let telephone voice mail provide a screen.

♦ Media receive a tremendous amount of material in the form of press releases, query letters, press kits and other information; that makes it difficult to gain their attention.

♦ Editorial space or broadcast time may be at a premium for many outlets. Therefore, they use less material, and yours needs to be on target for their needs.

The challenge, therefore, is how to cut through the "new-clutter" of the technology-driven communications era to foster good will and enhance relationships that open opportunities to get "the ear" of editors about your company's story.

The effective use of carefully selected promotional products can help. Promotional products used as inexpensive, non-obligatory business gifts are proved as an attention-getter and goodwill-builder.

This is not to suggest you indiscriminately give products to editors. Rather, include them in a carefully crafted campaign to focus attention to your material that crosses an editor's desk:

♦　　The dimensional aspect of the mailing will gain more attention and encourage the recipient to open it.

♦　　As a useful item, the promotional product will be retained and used by the media person; the imprint provides a desk-top sign for your company or product -- an advantage over your competitors.

♦　　Because it's useful, it is appreciated, enhancing recall of your mailing at the time you contact the editor to discuss your project.

The following examples of successful uses of promotional campaigns to communicate with media provide ideas you can adapt:

♦　　S-B Power Tool: Trade shows provide an excellent forum for companies to introduce products and executives to the various media attending the show. Meetings with editors often result in favorable publicity that can showcase a product, setting it apart from the competition and generating sales lead inquiries.

The task to schedule meetings can be formidable. Editors have limited time available to visit exhibits. Prior to a show, they are inundated with invitations, calls, news releases and press kits. The challenge for the inviter is to create an invitation method that's memorable, has a theme related to the message being sent *and* is useful to the recipient.

S-B Power Tool Company, marketer of *Skil* and *Bosch* brand power tools, used that formula to set appointments with 40 trade and consumer magazine editors at the National Hardware Show in Chicago. The nucleus of the invitation was a pre-paid phone card good for 15 minutes of free long distance calling time. The vinyl wallet-sized card was imprinted with a specially designed logo showing silhouettes of S-B's products. The reverse side included instructions for placing a call through an 800-number.

Cards were mailed with a cover letter that stated, in part, "Give us a few minutes of your time to learn about our products and we'll give you 15 minutes of free calling time."

Missing from the cards was the Personal Identification Number (PIN) required to activate the call. The letter advised that the PIN would be given at the show booth. Follow-up calls were made to each recipient. Ninety-five percent recalled the mailing.

Eighty-three percent kept their appointments and, of those, 75 percent had the phone card with them. PINs were mailed after the show to all media on the invitation list that did not receive them at the show.

Summarizing the program, Sil Argentin, S-B's manager of marketing communications said, "The benefits of this mailing included the high recall that aided in follow-up conversations, the high percentage of participation in the delayed fulfillment aspect and the positive perception editors had of phone cards as an item useful to them."

♦ Hauser-Ross Eye Institute: Local media were invited, along with civic leaders, previous patients and the community at large, to an open house to introduce the firm's new cataract surgery center in Sycamore, Ill.

Included with the invitation sent to media were two promotional products slated for distribution to guests following a guided tour of the facility during the open house event. One item was a purse-sized mirror in a vinyl holder imprinted with the theme "Opening the Doors to Better Vision," and the center's phone number. The other product was a soft plastic key tag imprinted with the institute's logo and phone number on one side and a miniature eye chart spelling out the clinic's name on the other side. A card, which read, "Thank you for sharing this special day as we open the doors to better vision," was included with each item.

♦ Jameson Home Products: The company wanted to gain media attention at the National Home Center Show for its new smoke alarm that was half the size of comparable alarms on the market. The theme, "Measure the Difference," was created to help visualize the size difference between the newly styled alarm and those of competitors.

A letter inviting editors to a press conference was sent, along with a tape measure imprinted, "Measure the Difference -- CODE ONE 2000." All major media represented at the show sent a representative to the conference.

16

Hints to Handle Media in Time of Crisis

Your company never has had a crisis and you can't imagine that it ever will.

Think again about the impact one of these situations can have on your business: murder, fire (especially with a loss of life), explosion, a hostage situation, a labor dispute or strike, a picket line set up by activists, a plant closing, an embezzlement, a major layoff, a natural disaster (tornado, earthquake, flood, hurricane) that destroys part or all of your facility, a lawsuit.

Each year, every one of these situations happens to businesses -- both large and small. Any such occurrence is guaranteed to gain the immediate attention of the media.

How do you handle the situation? First, remember that the job of reporters is to get the story. They'll do that with or without your cooperation.

The risk of being uncooperative, however, is that the story can be based on hearsay, rumor and misinformation from outside sources. Such a story most often can be damaging to your company and its reputation.

Conversely, when communicated to honestly, editors will tend to write the facts, and the attention to the crisis in the press can subside quickly.

It's best to prepare *before* a catastrophic event -- have a written plan of action to implement should a disaster occur. The plan need not be elaborate; it should include the following information:

♦ A list of individuals (and their day and night phone numbers) to be called immediately, including top management, the public relations director and the public relations agency if you have one.

♦ A list of executives authorized to speak with the media. It's a good idea to have an alternative in the event the primary source is unavailable.

♦ Include a media contact checklist that helps you decide actions: Are the media to be called? Is a press conference warranted? Does the situation call for merely responding to media inquiries? The decisions will be based, in part, on the severity of the situation and should be made jointly by top management and public relations counsel.

If calls are to be made, who will initiate those calls and what will be told to the media?

If a press conference is to be called, have a plan for disseminating the information quickly.

For incoming calls, who will talk to the reporters?

♦ Attach (and update periodically) a list of all media important to your company. In addition to local press, the list may include business journals, news wire services and trade publications.

♦ Attach a format for a media log to be used to record all incoming calls, the name of the media outlet, the reporter, time of call, who responded and comments.

Aside from pre-crisis preparation, the most important guidelines for communicating to media during a crisis are the following:

♦ Communicate promptly and frequently; don't try to suppress information.

♦ Be honest and forthright.

♦ Issue press releases and statements in writing. Try to limit verbal response, but when you must speak in response to queries, stick with the facts. Take care not to speculate or to say too much.

♦ Provide general background on the company so the reporter gets the facts correctly.

♦ Provide regular updates when there is a change in the situation.

♦ If you don't know the answer to a question, say so and tell the reporter you'll call back; then get the answer and call.

♦ When victims are involved, you can withhold release of names until next of kin have been notified.

♦ You don't have to allow reporters into the plant or site of a disaster. You should set up a nearby staging area if the situation dictates the media will be on the scene for a long period.

The publicity impact of a disaster can be minimized and laid to rest quickly by following these guidelines.

17

Some Media Relations Secrets

Here are some "secrets" about working with the media that you will not find in any textbook. In some cases, media will not even confess to these practices.

♦ **Media love to bandwagon**. That is, there are occasions when one media outlet covers a story, others will hop on the proverbial bandwagon and pursue the story.

Here's one real-life example. *The Wall Street Journal* ran a two-line item on the front page about a new auto air freshener from Gold Eagle Co. that can alter the moods of the driver and passengers. The blurb caught the attention of Chicago's leading morning drive time broadcaster Bob Collins of *WGN Radio*, who conducted a live 10-minute interview with a company executive that morning.

Soon thereafter, the *NBC* affiliate *WMAQ-TV* contacted the company and sent a reporter and video crew to Gold Eagle and produced a two-minute news segment. The producers felt the interview warranted a feed to all *NBC* affiliates across the country, many of which aired the segment.

What does this mean? Even the smallest placement in terms of size, or even media outlet, can spark significant coverage.

♦ **Media monitor other media**. As the above example shows, media watch, listen and view themselves. That means coverage in a local trade journal -- let's say one that covers food service and restaurants -- can provide the added benefit of reaching the reporter who covers the food service industry at the local newspaper.

Certainly, a marketing story in your local newspaper will be read by the marketing reporter at the regional business magazine. The Chicago bureau chief for *U.S. News & World Report* recently told a group of public relations professionals that he reads the Chicago newspapers, trade magazines and the journal *Chicago Enterprise* for story ideas.

♦ **You can't generalize about how media people prefer to work with you**. You will discover that an editor at one national business magazine prefers to hear story suggestions "pitched" over the phone, while an editor at a competitive business journal recommends faxes and refuses to take cold calls. Some broadcast producers opt for the pitch letter and a follow-up; others say send the letter, and "We'll call you if we're interested."

The "secret" to coping with this is really no secret at all. You need to learn the preferences and habits of the media you regularly contact, and respond to their needs and desires.

♦ **Offer story ideas to media that are not related to your organization or industry**. When you spot a situation with good story potential, even if the prospective story has nothing to do with the products or services you market, let the reporter or editor know about it via a letter or phone call. If the editor likes the idea, he or she may be more receptive the next time you pitch a story idea about your company.

♦ **You can -- and should -- build relationships with your key target media**. Many of the points in this chapter and others can go a long way toward achieving this. Know what your media targets cover; know what stories they have done; send them background, when appropriate, even if it doesn't pertain to a specific story idea; go out to breakfast or lunch just to background them on industry developments; and so on.

But always remember this. No matter how great the relationship...even if it's your favorite cousin who writes for the local newspaper...your story must have value to the reader, listener or viewer.

It's not who you know; it's offering the right information, in the right format...and at the right time.

Part Three

Tactics That Guarantee
a Successful Publicity Program

18

Writing the Basic News Release

In addition to media contact, distribution of news releases can generate press coverage and, in some cases, provide some very meaningful results.

This means someone -- maybe even you -- will have to write the prose and actually string some words together that form sentences -- and news!

Writing an effective, interesting and usable news release often forms the basis of many hours in the classroom...and lots of practice. What we're going to do here is just provide some essential guidelines:

♦   First, unlike a novel, in which the author saves the most important information for the last chapter, a news release must have the most vital facts in the lead and the next couple of paragraphs, with less important facts covered later in the release.

       This is called the inverted pyramid writing style. Picture a pyramid, but turn it upside down. Essential data fills out the top of the pyramid, while less crucial information filters down like a funnel.

       The news release or story is written that way because if the newspaper or magazine has limited space, the editor can easily cut from the bottom up, thereby leaving the key information in the article.

- Follow the newspaper style that answers the five W's and H -- who, what, when, where, why and how. Cover these high up in the story. You can expand on these points with more detail later in the release.

- Like the pitch letter, write concisely and keep paragraphs short.

- Your release presentation should be in a format acceptable to the media. This means the first page on company letterhead (other pages white); a contact name and phone number positioned in the right or left top corner of the first page; a headline; a release date; copy double spaced; enough room in the left and right margins for editors to make notes.

- Write in an objective style. When referring to your firm or organization, don't state "our company" or use the word "I" unless this is in a quote. It should read "the company." Also, avoid puffery, jargon, technical terms, editorial opinions. As Sgt. Joe Friday on *Dragnet* used to say, "Just the facts, ma'am."

- To help you organize the release, develop an outline first.

- Read your release out loud. Often it is easier to hear awkward-sounding phrases than to look for them on paper.

- Proofread, proofread, proofread. Be sure that the release does not contain a single typo and that names are spelled correctly, phone numbers are accurate and not transposed.

64

♦   Lastly...make sure your news release actually contains news! Some of those elements were discussed in the chapter on the pitch letter.

Remember, news for one media outlet may not be news in another, so it's difficult to generalize. What is newsworthy for the local community paper may not warrant a mention in the big city daily, and vice versa.

For example, a community paper may run a news story on a local resident that wins a company award, whereas the major daily may run a one line sentence or nothing at all. Conversely, a large daily would run a story on a company's annual national sales; for the community paper, this may not be "local" enough.

19

A Publicity Staple -- the Press Kit

A staple of many publicity programs is the media information, or press, kit.

The kit, essentially, is a folder with two inside pockets that contains news releases, photos, backgrounders and other materials that the media can use to provide coverage on your company or organization.

The cover of the folder, in some cases, is printed to feature the name of the organization. Other firms will create very elaborate covers with four-color graphics and special designs. One company in the appliance industry, for instance, created a folder to replicate a refrigerator/freezer.

A less expensive route is to purchase generic folders from an office supplies outlet and print the company name on a sticker for placement on the cover. Another route: Use your company's mailing label, type in the words "media kit" and place that on the cover.

Realistically, the media aren't as impressed with the way the kit folder looks; it's what inside that counts with them. So, what should be inserted?

The answer often is based on the planned use of the kit. Kits are frequently utilized:

♦ At trade shows, many of which have press rooms set aside primarily for exhibitors' press kits. Companies also should have a quantity available at their exhibit for media that visit the booth.

- At press conferences, for distribution to the media in attendance.

- Before and during executive interviews, to educate the reporter about the issues to be discussed and to serve as reference when the story is developed.

- In mailings to the media, particularly when contact is infrequent, or when a media relations program is conducted for the first time.

Most press kits contain:

- Releases on the latest news from your organization. Most often, the kits feature announcements on new products and/or services. Other news releases can announce new company developments (like a plant expansion, a new advertising program or an industry award), new executives or a company milestone (such as record sales or an anniversary).

- A fact sheet on your organization. This one- to two-page document provides a quick overview, covering such subjects as your firm's services and/or product lines, special innovations, corporate philosophy, history, headquarters location and plant cities and executive team.

- A feature story that reflects the company's products or service. For example, a company that markets a range of glues and adhesive products could include an article that provides consumers tips on selecting the best glue for the job. A commercial collection agency may include a story on how collecting money faster can improve company profits.

♦   Biographies of key executives.

♦   A list of article ideas that could assist media in identifying approaches to take for generating coverage.

♦   Black-and-white photos for media to use to illustrate the releases, stories and article ideas. Some firms include color slides in the kit. Since not all publications require color, you may opt to simply offer slides to media that request them.

♦   Existing printed materials on your organization. However, you should use such background judiciously to avoid transforming the information kit into a sales kit. A corporate brochure or annual report would be appropriate; a product flyer or two may be suitable. The bulk of the contents, however, should be editorial materials.

As with many of the guidelines for publicity activities, customization is the key for creating the ideal press kit.

The "forum" for its use and the media recipient will dictate the kit's contents.

20

The Camera-Ready News Release (or Going to the 'Mat')

A proven publicity-generating technique used for years by companies and public relations firms alike is the camera-ready news release.

Old-time public relations pros remember when this was called the mat release due to its actual physical form when sent to newspapers. The mat would be in the form of "hot type" that could be easily accommodated by the printing press.

Today, the release is in the form of a repro proof that newspapers simply place on their layouts, using the release as is. Some release distribution services today transmit these releases via Internet and CD-ROM, in addition to traditional mail.

Why should you supplement your media contact efforts with a camera-ready release...and pay an outside service to coordinate and distribute?

First, the economies involved are significant. The services will send your release to some 10,000 newspapers; in many instances (based on the size of the article), the total fee is less than the cost of just the postage. The price also covers the duplication of the release. And, if a photo is reprinted, just think of the added cost of 7,000 photos.

In most cases, your release will not be edited because the papers will pick up the camera ready story as is.

And, yes, newspapers seek and utilize these materials. Most of the top 500 daily newspapers publish camera-ready releases and nearly all of the 1,060 other dailies and 8,450 weeklies use the stories.

Why? The smaller papers do not have the staff to write many feature stories or cover lifestyle topics such as food, health, consumerism and the like. The writers are too busy covering the news in their respective towns.

The large dailies, also suffering from reduced staffs, have become frequent users of the releases, particularly when publishing special themed sections such as gardening, back-to-school, or holiday gifts.

As always, usage will be dictated by the news value of the release, its timeliness, the quality of the writing and the benefit to the reader.

It's a tactic worth considering, especially if your company markets nationally.

21

Radio Actualities --
Publicity Power Through the Airwaves

Radio is a powerful medium. The successes of Rush Limbaugh, Larry King and others attest to that. Yet, radio often is overlooked when conducting a publicity program, even though it can be an extremely cost-effective tactic.

Of course, there are the typical approaches for gaining radio coverage, talk show appearances or news broadcast interviews. Another successful method is producing your own news segment with the help of a professional broadcast service.

You've heard many such voice "actualities," but perhaps never thought about how they occurred, or the fact that you or your organization's spokesperson can be interviewed.

Here's how radio actualities work:

♦ A suitable news topic is selected.

♦ Your spokesperson comments as an authoritative source.

♦ A professional broadcast service interviews the person live or by phone.

♦ The broadcaster "surrounds" the interviewee's comments with a news-related opening and closing, resulting in a segment running about one minute long.

♦ The broadcaster phones radio station newsrooms, which tape the segment for later broadcast.

In some cases, the actual interview is recorded and tape cassettes are mailed to radio stations, particularly if the topic is not time sensitive.

Such distribution can be on a city-by-city, regional or national basis, depending on your objectives. Many times, actualities can be aired on national and regional networks, increasing coverage significantly. The numbers can be substantial, reaching as many as five, 10 and even 15 million listeners.

Some examples:

♦ The cities of Chicago, Milwaukee and Minneapolis were the targets when Ford Motor Company wanted to draw attention to its exhibit at the auto shows in those towns. An interview with the editor of *Motor Trend* extolled the virtues of the Ford Thunderbird, selected by the magazine as "Car of the Year." The interview was distributed prior to the shows in each market, with a different lead-in noting the dates and location of the event. In Chicago, 29 stations accepted the interview, Milwaukee gained 31 acceptances and 18 stations took the interview in Minneapolis.

♦ Promotional Products Association International sought to inform business people that giving inexpensive gifts can help cement business relationships, increase sales and serve as door openers. Proof of these benefits was gained in a study by Arizona State University. An interview with the professor who conducted the research was accepted by 1,540 stations, including the 927-station Mutual Network.

74

♦ Keebler Co. wanted to support a national point-of purchase display promotion that offered a large stuffed bear as a holiday gift, tied to the firm's sponsorship of the movie, *Miracle On 34th Street*. An interview with the company's brand manager provided details on the program, and a tape cassette mailing aired on 273 stations, reaching 6.2 million listeners.

In addition to consumer and business audiences, actualities can target specialized markets such as African Americans, Hispanics, sports-oriented audiences and other special interest groups.

22

Satellite Media Tours --
How to Reach Massive TV Audiences

Half of the American public, approximately 130 million people, look to television for *all* of their news. They do not read newspapers or news magazines. They are not reached through words, but through pictures, video footage and broadcast interviews.

To reach this massive audience, many companies participate in Satellite Media Tours (SMTs) to deliver their messages in a timely, credible and cost-effective way. Here's why:

♦ Regular traveling media tours are expensive and time consuming.

♦ SMTs can target stations in your key markets.

♦ Unlike Video News Releases, station bookings let you know your results in advance.

Instead of having your spokesperson spend days or weeks on the road meeting with target media face-to-face, all interviews can occur on one day from one studio locale.

By making sure you have a timely, interesting subject to discuss, some in-studio visuals and/or B-roll footage, the SMT can reach a vast audience.

It works this way. Television and cable stations are informed about the SMT topic and spokesperson days before the SMT. They then reserve time to conduct a brief 10-minute interview with the spokesperson via satellite.

During the SMT, your spokesperson remains in a comfortable studio while television stations across the country are "beamed in" electronically to conduct the interviews.

To illustrate, several companies introducing new products at a National Hardware Show partnered and used the show as the news peg for the SMT.

They enlisted as a spokesperson do-it-yourself writer and TV show host, Beverly DeJulio. She spoke with one national cable TV station and 15 local network affiliate stations. In each interview, she profiled the new products just unveiled by the SMT corporate sponsors.

As a result, more than 21 stations in 18 U.S. markets, including Chicago, Washington D.C., Detroit and Dallas, broadcast interviews with DeJulio.

The cost and type of coverage could not be matched. A typical SMT reaches approximately 12 markets per half day. Spot advertisements in those 12 markets would cost much more than what sponsors paid to participate in the SMT.

But more importantly, SMT spots represent editorial coverage and, to consumers, have more credibility than advertising because of its implied third-party (media) endorsement.

23

Polls Produce Publicity

Perhaps *USA Today's* "snapshot" box demonstrates it best: Media love statistics. The front pages of the national newspaper include some interesting "numbers" each day.

Other frequent users of interesting figures range from *The Wall Street Journal* to local radio and television news commentators.

The sources for much of this published data are the public relations departments of corporations or the agencies that serve them. They have discovered that sponsoring a survey -- and reporting its results -- is one effective approach to gaining media coverage.

Plus, the sponsor of the survey is positioned as an authoritative source of information and can build this image through publicity in trade and consumer media.

The beauty of the tactic is that you don't have to hire a Gallup or Roper to conduct expensive research and interview 1,000 or more people. You can generate a statistically-oriented story by polling a specific audience on topics that, when analyzed, will produce information of news value. Media accept survey results based on respondents that may number only 100. Polls do differ from full-scale research surveys in that no attempt is made to project the results on a national basis. Rather, the technique provides opinion only from small, well-defined market segments.

Usually, between 100 to 200 people are asked four to eight questions, either in person, by phone or by mail, as the situation dictates.

For instance, trade shows offer a good platform because the audience usually is "homogeneous," providing a group of people with a similar demographic, economic or industry profile.

Here are three examples of "publicity polls" recently conducted:

♦ A power tool manufacturer surveyed home builders at the National Association of Home Builders convention on their feelings about the key attributes of power tools. *Associated Press* covered the findings, as did numerous industry trade journals.

♦ A public relations firm polled office workers in a downtown plaza regarding the frequency of eating snacks and lunch at their desks. The results indicated that many employees are "desk potatoes" and the story made *USA Today*, the front page of the *Detroit News*, the *Chicago Sun-Times*, among others.

♦ A survey mailed to executives on behalf of a trade group in the promotions industry revealed an astounding number of the managers adorned their offices with imprinted promotional products, which netted coverage in leading marketing journals and newspapers coast to coast.

Simplicity and speed make informal polls an effective way to generate publicity. One final tip: Before developing the survey, think about the kind of lead to the story you seek. It will help you create the questions...and generate results that will be newsworthy.

24

PR Maximizes Trade Show Investment

Companies spend thousands upon thousands of dollars to exhibit at trade shows, yet many fail to maximize *return on investment.*

Trade show success usually is measured in terms of orders received, leads generated, contacts maintained or customers entertained. Often ignored is the value-added bonus public relations can achieve.

Two areas in which public relations techniques can enhance trade show participation are media relations and pre-show promotion.

Publicity is much more cost-effective than advertising as a way to gain attention among trade show attendees and, at the same time, reach prospects who do not attend. Proven techniques:

♦ Provide trade publications with information far enough in advance to be included in special show editions. Reprint the published stories to use as a hand-out to visitors at your exhibit.

♦ Develop a complete media information kit detailing your company and products for placement in the press room at the show.

♦ If there is news about your company, or a truly unique new product introduction, notify local media in advance of the show. A company that unveiled an unbreakable window glass invited media to attempt to break the glass with a baseball bat. Local newspapers and TV stations carried the story the morning the show opened, gaining the attention of convention attendees and increasing visits to the exhibit.

♦ If consumers are a target, radio is an effective way to highlight your product. An interview, referred to as an "actuality," of a company spokesperson can be pre-recorded and electronically transmitted locally, regionally or nationally when the show opens. This takes advantage of the timely news value of the show.

♦ Conduct an informal poll at your exhibit of 100 to 150 attendees on an industry-related topic, develop and distribute a news release based on the findings, gaining credit as the sponsor of the "survey."

♦ Build relationships with the media by scheduling appointments with editors to visit your exhibit and meet with top executives. Don't succumb to the temptation to hold a press conference unless your "news" warrants it.

Devcon, a producer of adhesive products, enjoyed individual visits by 30 reporters over a two-day period at its Hardware Show exhibit. Prior to the show, reporters were informed by letter and phone that a "Stick To Your Ribs" gourmet box lunch would be given to them at the booth following a briefing on new "sticky" Devcon products.

- ♦ "Guarantee" qualified attendance at your exhibit through pre-show promotion. A survey reported in *Sales & Marketing Management* magazine noted that less than 6 percent of exhibitors use any form of pre-show promotion. One company reached attendees during a show by simply printing a special newsletter that was slipped under the doors of hotel guest rooms.

Trade show participation is expensive. As the battle for mindshare at trade shows intensifies, the need to maximize the investment becomes more urgent. Public relations is a comparatively inexpensive response to that need.

25

Spokespersons Can Add Spark to Publicity Programs

All of us recognize the advertising power of the celebrity spokesperson. Hellooooooo, Michael Jordan!

The spokesperson also can play a role in powering a publicity program. However, while a "celebrity" can help, an outside spokesperson who represents your organization to the editorial media must have a natural link to your product or service, or be an expert, such as a professor, doctor or industry guru.

Why use a spokesperson? An outside expert can lend credibility to your message...and if this person is a well-known personality to boot, media attention usually increases as well.

These illustrations reveal how a spokesperson can help spark coverage:

- Alleviating stress is one of the benefits of relaxing in an elaborate whirlpool tub. To reinforce this message, Kohler Co. enlisted a University of Chicago professor who had just published a book on stress management to speak to the press when the new line of whirlpools was unveiled at a New York press conference.

- Brown Shoe Co. sponsored the creation of walking paths in several major U.S. cities. To emphasize the benefits of walking, keeping your legs in shape and wearing comfortable shoes, the firm hired famed dancer Cyd Charisse to officially open each path, attend store events and convey key messages to the media.

♦ To educate children about the dangers of drugs, Keebler Co. created and traveled to shopping malls a puppet show that addressed the issue. Spokesperson for the tour was the key consultant to The White House Drug Abuse Policy Office.

♦ The personification of high fashion for men -- actor George Hamilton -- extolled the benefits of sole leather shoes in media interviews for the Sole Leather Council.

♦ A sensitive topic -- the purchase of monuments for deceased family members -- was addressed delicately yet authoritatively for the monument industry association by a doctor who specialized in bereavement counseling.

♦ Do-it-yourself expert and "Hometime" TV host Dean Johnson served as the media spokesperson for Kohler Co.'s "Remodeling America" exhibit that toured the country and educated homeowners on the benefits of remodeling their kitchens and baths.

26

Get Creative --
Enhance Your Publicity Results

The basic recipe for publicity success discussed in these chapters always can be enhanced with a dash of creativity.

You say you're not creative? Really, everyone possesses some of that flair. If it's not exhibited at work, maybe you staged a party at home with an unusual theme, selected an imaginative gift for a friend or even wrote memorable vows for your wedding.

Applying some of that thought and talent to your publicity program can bring more life, excitement and, ultimately, added editorial coverage. Here are just a few examples:

- ♦ What can be more routine than showing executives holding shovels for a groundbreaking photo to announce a new building? Instead, the Northern Trust Bank in Winnetka, Ill., enlisted the children of bank employees to dig up the ground with toy trucks and shovels to herald the event...and placed the unusual photo on the *Associated Press* wire.

- ♦ Mustard may be one of the most mundane of products. Yet, makers of French's mustard developed an unusual concept -- the winter picnic -- and staged one in Central Park for food editors at national consumer magazines. Broadcast as well as print publicity was gained.

♦ Accounts receivables management firm Mid-Continent Agencies, always developing stories that provide tips on cash flow and avoiding debt, sought a new angle. MCA created profiles of your typical credit card abusers (such as Depression Spenders, Binge Buyers and Credit Card Collectors), prepared a story on the profiles and weaved in its messages. Magazines, wire services and newspapers across the country ran the article.

♦ The president of leading brownie maker Plantation Baking created controversy -- and coverage -- when he proclaimed in a news release, and supported with facts, that the brownie was more American than apple pie. The timing of the story? Two weeks before July 4.

♦ The "knights" from Medieval Times, a medieval-themed dinner theater complex outside Chicago, simply walked in to several radio stations with a flower and love poem to present to women disc jockeys on Valentine's Day. These acts of chivalry on that special day were reported by several stations, including market leader *WGN*.

♦ To boost awareness of its traditional, ordinary oatmeal product, Quaker Oats conducted an amusing survey to identify who were morning people...and who were not. One solution to be a better morning person? Eat a good breakfast (and oatmeal).

You don't need to generate the creative sparks in a vacuum. You could gather a few co-workers together and brainstorm some new approaches. Or, subscribe to one of the public relations trade journals for ideas. Another great tactic: Watch for "publicity stunts" that appear in the media...probably on a daily basis.

Part Four

Case Histories --
Ideas You Can Use

Case History

Electronistore Services, Inc.

OBJECTIVES

Perhaps the most difficult challenge facing a start-up company marketing a new concept is to find a way to demonstrate to prospects the value and benefits of its product in a credible, tangible method.

Such was the hurdle that had to be overcome by Electronistore Services, Inc., Chicago. This new subsidiary of a major commercial printer was formed to produce and market the first interactive electronic shopping system designed specifically to meet the needs of retailers. Called Electronistore, the system featured the most advanced, interactive electronic shopping hardware and software available and provided retailers with extensive selling flexibility and consumer marketing information.

Although industry sources predicted a high rate of transactional electronic shopping units in retail locations in the United States, Electronistore, as a pioneer, found a marketplace that had little understanding of such systems and their benefits.

Beyond the initial announcement about the creation of Electronistore, gaining publicity for the company and its systems was extremely difficult. There were no units in stores that media could see. In addition, there were no endorsements the company presently could use -- either from customers or the media -- to provide a sense of confidence and to communicate the value of the concept to prospective clients. Without this marketing ammunition, retailers were reluctant to initiate discussions with Electronistore and explore in-depth the opportunities open to them through adopting the Electronistore system in their operations.

Electronistore did have one ace -- its first customer, E&B Marine, Inc., was scheduled to install the system in eight of its 25 retail outlets in the eastern United States.

Electronistore felt the E&B introduction could provide the solution to its major marketing problem -- the lack of a credible third-party endorsement to support the company's basic promotional and advertising materials. Public relations strategy was based on this unprecedented opportunity in the firm's brief history to develop the desperately needed sales materials.

TECHNIQUES

The first display of the system was to occur at E&B's exhibit at the huge Miami International Boat Show. Use of this event would give Electronistore an earlier and better opportunity to gain the needed tangible endorsements from its first customer.

It was determined that this endorsement be created through media coverage of E&B's unveiling of its Electronistore system, called the Marine Accessory Center. The strategy suggested was to use E&B's chairman as the spokesperson in media interviews arranged during the show, an ideal news platform for media.

The approach was not to gain publicity for publicity's sake. The key element in this plan was to take any media coverage attained and, from it, produce printed and visual materials for use by the Electronistore sales staff to reinforce the messages they take to prospects.

The Miami International Boat Show is one of the largest of its kind in this country and the third largest in the world. There is intense competition for media attention from the hundreds of exhibitors, which include all the leading boat manufacturers and producers of boating products usually more innovative and impressive than those offered by a supplies retailer such as E&B Marine. It was decided to approach the media with a different twist to the exhibition. E&B informed the editors and broadcast producers that the most interesting display at the show was not one featuring new boating products, but a revolutionary way to shop for them.

Based on this story line, an intense effort was conducted to arrange interviews and to schedule demonstrations of the system for media.

RESULTS

The media coverage gained at the show for E&B's system provided the materials from which to produce the long-sought marketing and sales materials. These materials were culled from 12 minutes of television broadcast time on three stations, 49 minutes of radio interview time and a major newspaper article. They included:

- ♦ A five-minute videotape highlighting the major, positive statements about the system made by E&B executives during three separate interviews on stations *WLRN-TV, WSVS-TV* and *WPLG-TV*, all in Miami.

- ♦ Printed excerpts of newspaper and television quotes displayed on 15-inch by 20-inch board enlargements.

- ♦ An 8 1/2-inch by 11-inch reprint of the same excerpts noted above.

- ♦ Reprints of the lengthy business page newspaper feature from the *Fort Lauderdale News/Sun Sentinel*.

- ♦ Cassettes of two radio interviews on stations *WIOD* and *WNWS*, both in Miami.

Electronistore used the materials at trade shows attended by retailing, merchandising and direct marketing executives, in direct mail and, most importantly, in personal one-to-one presentations made by Electronistore's top management.

Electronistore's national sales manager reported, "Through these materials, we can have prospects share the excitement of the atmosphere created when this entrepreneurial leader introduced the interactive shopping system designed and produced by our firm. These are powerful tools that we believe are invaluable in our selling process."

Case History

Mama Tish's Enterprises, Ltd.

OBJECTIVES

A Chicago-based "David" among the "Goliaths" in the frozen fruit gourmet dessert industry, Mama Tish's Enterprises, Ltd., identified a need to accelerate its marketing efforts to keep pace in the growing and fierce battle for grocery freezer space and consumer acceptance for such products.

Although the manufacturer of Mama Tish's Gourmet Sorbetto (fresh fruit ices) had achieved steady growth since its founding, its chairman knew a stronger push was needed to ensure the product was not "frozen out" by grocers both locally and in other targeted U.S. markets.

The company faced stiff competition from a number of food service giants. Firms such as Dole's, Welches and Minute Maid had jumped on the bandwagon of consumer acceptance of frozen fruit products, had introduced new lines of frozen novelty products and supported these new offerings with extensive advertising and promotional dollars. Limited marketing funds was yet another obstacle Mama Tish's had to overcome in this uphill struggle.

The ambitious objectives set for the program to be conducted over a nine-month period were to:

♦   Gain a stronger share in the firm's home market -- Chicago -- by communicating to the grocery trade and consumers what Mama Tish's felt was its major competitive edge -- its all-natural, fresh fruit product that is practically sodium- and cholesterol-free.

95

- Generate objective, third-party endorsement of the product that could be utilized by Mama Tish's in sales presentations before grocery store buyers both in Chicago and in target markets.

- Contribute to Mama Tish's efforts to raise capital by using these positive endorsements to attract investors when the firm conducted a planned private stock offering.

TECHNIQUES

What would serve as Mama Tish's "slingshot" in its battle with the giants?

It was decided to take advantage of two key Mama Tish's strengths: 1) its Chicago roots and solid presence in the Windy City, and 2) the supreme confidence Mama Tish's executives possessed in the product, which "fulfills the fruit lover's fantasy."

With these strengths serving as themes, a corporate and product publicity program was directed solely to Chicago media in an effort to generate the needed endorsements. And, promotional tie-in opportunities were sought that required minimal cash investment from Mama Tish's to further spark consumer awareness.

But gaining media attention for a five-year-old dessert product required a number of bold approaches. The biggest gamble, yet one that produced the greatest payoff, was a proposal to the food editors at the *Chicago Sun-Times* to match Mama Tish's Gourmet Sorbetto against all others in an independent taste test. The glories of sorbetto were heralded in the lead story in the *Sun-Times* food section, highlighted by the paper's taste test that announced Mama Tish's as the "hands-down winner." The section also featured a profile on the firm.

Could Mama Tish's gain the attention of Chicago's divergent radio personalities? On a searing, hot July day, Mama Tish's delivered a case of its gourmet sorbetto to the leading

96

afternoon drive-time DJs with an invitation to cool off with the fresh fruit ices. At least four DJs extolled the virtues of the product on the air. One DJ discussed the product over a 25-minute span.

How about the business press? Mama Tish's battle to gain market share with no advertising and its dreams to take this family recipe from Taylor Street to the rest of the country were bolstered by lengthy business features in the *Chicago Tribune* and the *Chicago Sun-Times*.

Two cost-effective summer-time promotions were arranged to provide further visibility. One involved radio station *WYTZ* and its special van that traveled to high traffic, public locations on five, three-day weekends. Samples of Mama Tish's were distributed free of charge by the *WYTZ* mobile van. In addition to this product sampling, the station provided Mama Tish's $25,000 in promotional air time value that announced the sorbetto giveaway and highlighted the product.

The second promotion also produced high-level awareness of the product. The Bank of Commerce held Sorbetto Days every Wednesday in August, giving away the product to passersby in exchange for donations to radio personality Wally Phillips' Neediest Children's Fund. In exchange for the free sorbetto provided by Mama Tish's, the company was promoted on Phillips' *WGN* radio program, in Bank of Commerce press releases and through prominent signage in the bank's outdoor plaza fronting North Michigan Avenue.

RESULTS

The pertinent factors to measure the effectiveness and value of the Mama Tish's program do not dwell on the number of publicity impressions generated nor the advertising equivalent of the editorial space and air time. Instead, measurement must be based on the quality of the media exposure, and how Mama Tish's merchandised this coverage to its important audiences.

The marketing of the *Sun-Times* taste test alone has been a major element in the firm's sales effort and successes. Reprints of this article were provided to every sales prospect and blowups of the article were displayed at every trade show Mama Tish's attended. The most significant use of the test is the creation of a chart portraying the results, which was a key component of the firm's dramatic sales kit and folder. The company's vice president of sales stated, "The chart depicting the taste-test results is the most convincing sales tool we have. It's not Mama Tish's promoting the qualities of its product, but an independent and prominent news source."

Reprints of the major articles were included in the information package distributed to potential investors in the firm. The taste-test story plus the positive business articles from the *Tribune* and *Sun-Times* played a major role in gaining participation in the private offering.

The articles helped reinforce the decision of the Dominick's Finer Foods grocery chain to stock Mama Tish's for the first time and continue to provide added freezer space for the product throughout the year.

The materials served as ideal door openers as the Mama Tish's sales force attempted to create new markets. And, in Chicago, the publicity contributed to growing consumer purchases, according to Mama Tish's executives. Sales locally increased 54 percent. A Nielsen Trend Report indicated Mama Tish's during one month outsold frozen novelties such as Dove Bar, Jello Fruit Bars, Chiquita Fruit Bars, Haagen Daz Bars and Klondike Bars -- without the support of advertising or in-store promotional programs or the benefit of a renowned national name.

It just took a "slingshot" filled with a top quality product and significant editorial endorsements.

Case History

Medieval Times

OBJECTIVES

The outdoor summer concert season was about to experience a terrible year.

The hospitality industry struggled, and the travel business was stuck in neutral.

Restaurants were fighting for survival. And even the American entertainment icon -- Disney World -- experienced attendance declines.

1991 assuredly was *not* the best time to open a $16 million entertainment attraction in Chicagoland. Yet, plans proceeded to unveil in June Medieval Times in Schaumburg, Ill., a "medieval" castle edifice that featured knights on horseback competing in tournament games and jousts in a large arena, surrounded and cheered by 1,400 spectators who dined medieval style (sans silverware).

The poor economy was not the only obstacle to success for Medieval Times:

- ◆ Although other Medieval Times castles existed in Florida, California and New Jersey, name recognition in Chicago was practically nil and the concept of a dinner tournament complex a mystery.

- ◆ Chicago lacked geographic advantages the other castles possessed. The New Jersey facility draws from a metropolitan area twice the size of Chicago, while the California and Florida castles are near major tourist attractions.

♦ As Medieval Times president Andres Gelabert told *Crain's Chicago Business*, "We won't spend big dollars on advertising." Only "fringe" TV spots and limited newspaper ads were purchased. Unlike attractions such as amusement parks, sports stadiums and even theaters, advertising would not serve as the attention-getter. Publicity would have to be the driving force to generate interest, attendance and sales.

The following were the objectives established to herald the new Medieval Times throughout the Chicago-area kingdom:

♦ Create and maintain awareness of Medieval Times among Chicago-area residents. Communicate the excitement and fun of traveling back in time to experience the romance of medieval chivalry, the skills of horsemanship and the pageantry of dining with nobility.

♦ Build this presence through a diverse range of editorial coverage that would entice Chicagoans to experience Medieval Times.

♦ In the crucial three-month start-up period, gain maximum attendance to foster widespread word-of-mouth endorsement. "Every person who comes to the show becomes our agent," Gelabert said, a major reason for the concept's success in other cities.

♦ Help Medieval Times attain its first year attendance goal.

TECHNIQUES

To obtain the scope of editorial coverage to both fill in the advertising gap and convince value-conscious Midwesterners to spend $25 to $35 a person for an unusual night out required intensive media relations activities:

♦ Television coverage was vital since visuals best conveyed and sold the dinner/tournament concept. To gain exposure on as many Chicago stations as possible required presenting different angles to each; it was suggested to specific producers that:

♦♦ *WLS-TV*'s "Chicago Stories" program focus on a day and night in the life of a knight.

♦♦ *WMAQ-TV*'s Norman Mark experience training as a knight.

♦♦ *WLS-TV*'s Frank Mathie report on the building of a castle.

♦♦ *WGN-TV* use Medieval Times as a "Chicago's Very Own" segment.

♦♦ *WTTW* ("Wild Chicago) and *WFLD-TV* ("9:30") report on the rather bizarre concept and antics of the knights and spectators.

♦ The opening of Medieval Times represented a major business story; business page articles were arranged for publication prior to, or coincidental to, the castle's opening, including the *Chicago Tribune* and *Crain's Chicago Business*.

♦ A variety of print and broadcast media were invited to experience the Medieval Times extravaganza and report to their readers/listeners. Included were restaurant/theater critics, travel writers, feature reporters, radio DJs.

- Knights were interviewed on radio and discussed their unusual jobs.

- Unusual photo opportunities were arranged, such as the knights preparing their swords for battle.

- Ongoing special feature stories were arranged and news announcements prepared covering:

  - The search for food service employees, called serfs and wenches.
  - Knights in training.
  - The first Chicagoan hired as a knight.
  - The castle's Michelangelo.
  - The castle's torture chamber.
  - The unusual medieval artifacts sold in the gift shop.

CREATIVITY

Examples of creative story suggestions and interview/news release topics included:

- A segment, "A Day and a Night in the Life of Medieval Times Knights," proposed to *WLS-TV*, that led to a 30-minute "Chicago Stories" program solely on the topic.

- Ben Hollis was "convinced" that Medieval Times and his "Wild Chicago" program were a perfect match.

- Knight Sir John visited radio stations on Valentine's Day to present flowers to female DJs and a love poem, read on the air to Kathy O'Malley on *WGN*.

- A knight escorted ladies across Michigan Avenue, photographed and published in the *Chicago Sun-Times* two days before the castle's opening.

RESULTS

Editorial coverage in the six-county Chicago metro area from June through March helped make Medieval Times a known entity, communicated the entertainment value of this unusual attraction and helped exceed attendance expectations.

- During the first three months of operation, Medieval Times was filled to 90-95 percent capacity, thereby generating in this crucial opening period tremendous word-of-mouth "exposure" -- a key communications objective.

- Through March 1992, some 300,000 people had attended Medieval Times performances, surpassing the first year goal 2 1/2 months before the first anniversary.

- If an equivalent amount of the print and broadcast coverage had been purchased as advertising, the cost would have been $294,674, more than 8.5 times the sum budgeted for public relations.

- Total broadcast time exceeded 61 minutes; more than 1,635 column inches of coverage generated.

A sampling of the publicity highlights includes:

- The 30-minute "Chicago Stories" program on *WLS-TV* focused solely on the Medieval Times knights.

♦ Additional Chicago TV coverage on *WMAQ, WGN, WLS, WFLD* and *WTTW*.

♦ The cover of *Chicago Sun-Times'* "Weekend Plus" section featured an illustration of a knight on horseback spearing a piece of chicken. Extensive Medieval Times coverage appeared inside.

♦ Major business article coverage in *Crain's Chicago Business* (with color photos), *Chicago Tribune*, *Daily Herald* and *Adweek*.

♦ Extensive print coverage on the Medieval Times experience was written by reporters attending performances. Stories appeared in Chicago and Illinois newspapers such as the *Chicago Tribune, Daily Herald, Rockford Register Star, Copley Newspapers* in Joliet, Waukegan, Elgin, Aurora and Wheaton, *La Raza*, Park Ridge/Des Plaines *Times Herald, River North News, Chicago Shoreland News*.

♦ Chicago radio coverage that included lengthy commentary by *WGN*'s Bob Collins: "It's a terrific show." *WLUP*'s Kevin Matthews said, "I highly recommend this." *WBBM-FM*'s Joe Bohanan noted, "It's a beautiful building."

Case History

Mid-Continent Agencies

OBJECTIVES

Why would an accounts receivable management firm wish to educate the public on how to avoid debt and credit card abuse? After all, the more consumers who are unable to pay bills, the better the business for the collections company.

Yet, boosting business was not the objective for Mid-Continent Agencies, Inc. (MCA) of Rolling Meadows, Ill., when it embarked on a three-month effort to alert Americans to the problems of rampant spending and to offer advice on controlling this nearly universal urge. Instead, MCA, concerned about the high level of outstanding consumer debt in the United States, felt its role as one of the leading accounts receivable management firms would be to help alleviate, in some way, what company president Les Kirschbaum viewed as a growing economic crisis. Based on the firm's experience in contacting debt-plagued consumers daily, MCA could bring a powerful perspective to the problem.

A public relations program, directed toward consumers, was designed to meet these objectives:

- ♦ Create an awareness among consumers of the problems of overspending and an understanding of the "ease" of becoming a credit card abuser.

- ♦ Provide consumers background and guidance on how to become wiser, more responsible shoppers and spenders.

TECHNIQUES

It was decided that through the mass media -- with special emphasis on the national press and "national" newspapers (e.g., *Chicago Tribune, Los Angeles Times*) -- MCA's messages could be told to the greatest numbers of American consumers. In addition, it was felt that the effort, to achieve maximum impact and maintain momentum, should be implemented over a three-month period.

The timing, in this case, was a key element. The information was to be disseminated during the biggest shopping period of the year -- prior to and during the Christmas and Chanukah holidays. This, it was felt, would be beneficial for two reasons: 1) the media would be most receptive to covering the issue during this time, and 2) this was the time of year when most people, indeed, fall into the overspending trap.

Media coverage was to be gained in two ways:

♦ The development and distribution to media across the country of two news/feature stories. One was titled "Are You A Binge Buyer Or Depression Spender" that outlined the various types of credit card abusers. The second was titled "How To Survive Holiday Spending: Plan Purchases" and provided recommendations on budgeting a holiday shopping program.

♦ The scheduling of interviews for MCA president Kirschbaum on these issues with major media outlets and those media responding to the two feature articles.

These press materials were distributed in November and the media contact effort initiated one week prior to the biggest shopping day in this country -- the Friday after Thanksgiving.

106

CREATIVITY

The creation of the 10 credit card profiles, outlined concisely in a 2 1/2 page story, played a major role in generating media attention to the issue.

From a tactical standpoint, the launch and implementation of the program during the holiday shopping season proved to be a creative way to best use the limited financial resources allocated for the campaign.

RESULTS

Media coverage on the consumer debt and overspending issue, sparked by the information provided by MCA and Kirschbaum, was extensive. Based only on the press clippings received, some 113 newspaper articles reaching an estimated 11.3 million readers were published on the key topics in the three month period. In addition, 12 television and radio interviews with Kirschbaum occurred, communicating the messages to a broadcast audience of some nine million (three interviews were broadcast several times). Total reader/viewer/listener impressions were more than 20 million.

The vast audience reach, occurring solely in November and December, was attained through these kinds of media placements:

- An article in *USA Today*'s "MoneyTalk" column.

- A lengthy page one feature story in the *Los Angeles Times*, which distributed the article nationally over the *Los Angeles Times News Service*.

- An article in the *Philadelphia Inquirer*, distributed nationally over the *Knight-Ridder* wire and picked up by a number of major newspapers, including the *Chicago Tribune*.

- A story sent to newspapers over the *Gannett News Service*.

- Distribution of the holiday shopping release by *Associated Press*' Texas state bureau.

- Individual stories based on the releases and/or interviews with Kirschbaum published in major newspapers such as the *Chicago Sun-Times, Buffalo News, Detroit News, Orange County Register* and *Pittsburgh Press*, among others.

- Television interviews on *WBBM-TV, WLS-TV, WFLD-TV* (all Chicago), *WKBW*'s "A.M. Buffalo" program in Buffalo, N.Y. and *WKBW* News in Buffalo (where MCA has a regional office).

- Radio interviews on *WLS* and *WMAQ*, Chicago; *KYW*, Philadelphia; *WCKY*, Cincinnati; *WINK*, Ft. Meyers, Fla.; *WAMJ*, South Bend, Ind.; *WDWS*, Champaign, Ill.

This coverage met MCA's goals of educating the public. "We hope consumers who read and heard the messages act upon them," said Kirschbaum. "We're certainly not against credit -- as long as it is planned and managed properly."

Case History

Promotional Products Association International

OBJECTIVES

The Promotional Products Association International (PPA), headquartered in Irving, Texas, is comprised of 5,500 members who are suppliers and distributors of imprinted promotional products.

PPA learned of an increase in deceptive direct marketing practices -- telephone or mail solicitation of business owners and managers by "boiler room" operators trying to sell low-quality products at inflated prices. Often, such products included imprinted promotional items, such as pens, which are lines coincidental to those sold by PPA-member firms.

The mission of "boiler-room" operators is to quickly turn over shoddy inventory, often purchased offshore at bargain basement prices. They lure unsuspecting business buyers with the promise of "valuable prizes," such as vacations, boats, real estate and appliances, provided the individual also agrees to purchase other products.

PPA was concerned that the reputation of its members would suffer from these scams because many members also sell through mail and phone direct marketing. Contact with the U.S. Postal Service, the Attorney General, the Federal Trade Commission and major credit card companies revealed a growing problem. Yet, while scams affecting the consumer public had been well publicized, very little was known that deceptive marketing was plaguing business executives.

109

The following objectives were established to combat the problem:

- ♦ Create among the business community an awareness of the proliferation of "boiler-room" practices, specifically those involving the sale of imprinted promotional products.

- ♦ Provide information useful to business executives in combatting such solicitations and encourage action to report incidents to proper authorities.

- ♦ Encourage buyers of business products to purchase from reputable direct marketers.

TECHNIQUES

A public service publicity campaign was aimed at business executives throughout the United States. The challenge to meet objectives on a limited project budget was met through the following techniques:

- ♦ A mail survey of business executives was conducted to gain facts to be used in the media campaign.

- ♦ A press conference was held at the PPA Convention in Dallas to report survey findings and to announce the public service education effort.

- ♦ During the convention, the PPA chairman of the board was interviewed by a radio news service firm; a one-minute segment was transmitted by phone contact to 1,600 radio stations nationally.

- ♦ A pamphlet, "The Boiler-Room Blues," was created as a primer on recognizing direct marketing scams and how to handle and report solicitations. The pamphlet, a photo of it with caption, a news release and a cover letter were distributed to national and regional business journals and marketing publications, suggesting the brochure be offered to readers through free literature columns. Copies of the pamphlet were made available free of charge by writing to PPA. More than 5,000 were distributed by the year's end.

♦ A newspaper mat story, "Deceptive Direct Marketing Tactics Deluge Business Executives," was written and distributed to 4,600 newspapers nationally. Included was a graphic depicting the key findings of the survey.

♦ Copies of all press materials and the pamphlet were distributed to the 30 regional promotional products associations for use in local market media contact as well as for individual members of the trade groups.

♦ PPA members were kept informed through periodic reports in the association's monthly publication, *Promotional Products Business*; members and non-member suppliers and distributors were informed through articles in an industry trade publication, *Counselor*.

♦ Copies of the materials were provided to authorities including the Federal Trade Commission and the Attorney General.

CREATIVITY

Prior to launching the campaign, it was decided to verify the magnitude of the problem and to obtain substantiation that could be brought to the target audience through the media. A mail survey of 500 business owners and managers yielded 130 responses. Results proved that "boiler-room" ploys were working too well:

- ♦ A whopping 85 percent reported they had been solicited by phone or mail by someone who informed them they won a valuable prize provided they also agreed to purchase other products.

- ♦ 22 percent contacted said they purchased products to receive the expensive gift offered.

- ♦ 64 percent reported the purchased products received were of inferior quality.

- ♦ 62 percent considered the merchandise overpriced.

- ♦ 7 percent said they never received the goods -- prize or products.

The results of the survey formed the basis for all media contact and a pamphlet, "The Boiler-Room Blues," which provided guidelines for recognizing and combatting direct marketing scams.

RESULTS

More than 30 million reader/viewer/listener impressions were gained. Beyond media coverage, however, positive results in meeting the objective to create awareness was gauged on the facts that PPA members reported value in their customer relations activities through use of article reprints and the pamphlet. And, while not specifically measured as a result of the program, PPA has noted that indictments of "boiler-room" operators increased.

Case History

S-B Power Tool Company

OBJECTIVES

Cordless power tools, perhaps the greatest innovation in the power tool category in the last quarter century, today are as common in the home workshop as saws, screws and sandpaper.

Therefore, when S-B Power Tool Company planned to unveil two new Skil brand cordless power tool lines, the impact among retailers, consumers and media -- if not communicated properly -- could be powerless in revving up sales.

The apparent appearance that these new cordless tools were just ho-hum additions to the burgeoning universe of power tools was not the only obstacle to meeting S-B's ambitious sales goals:

- ◆ The two lines -- the Flexi-Charge Interchangeable Power System and a line of 12-volt battery tools -- incorporated three Skil tools (the Twist Xtra Screwdriver, Super Twist Screwdriver and Top Gun Cordless Drill/Driver) introduced several years ago.

- ◆ Advertising support was limited, focused primarily on only a pre-holiday three-month TV ad program for Flexi-Charge and even fewer ad dollars for the 12-volt line.

- Competition in the power tool marketplace had become fierce, particularly from several Japanese companies and Black & Decker.

The public relations campaign was "charged" to overcome these roadblocks and meet these objectives:

- Create awareness among target audiences of this newest generation of cordless tools, their unique features and benefits.

- Position Flexi-Charge as the most innovative in the cordless power tool category.

- Achieve editorial dominance in the consumer media that reached targets despite the intense competition for editorial space among power tool manufacturers, filling the communications gap created by limited advertising.

- Help S-B attain its sales goals for the product lines.

TECHNIQUES

Meeting these objectives and sales targets, to be driven via editorial coverage, required a well-conceived plan enabling the Skil cordless tools to gain media attention, and through the media, interest and sales from retailers and end-users.

One essential tactic: stressing that Flexi-Charge did have some distinctions. It was the first broad line of cordless tools for consumers that featured the professional tool benefit of removable, rechargeable batteries that are easily recyclable, alleviating the dangerous disposal of nickel cadmium batteries in landfills. Plus, the 12-volt battery tools featured the first cordless Skilsaw circular saw on the market and environmental benefits similar to Flexi-Charge.

114

Strategies and techniques utilized included:

◆ Creation of communications vehicles that provided opportunities to convey that these power tools possessed an attribute all others do not -- they are environmentally friendly. Activities included:

  ◆◆ Establishing a battery collection program at Skil service centers throughout the country for all used batteries within Skil cordless tools. This underscored S-B's commitment to recycling batteries and the benefits of the cordless tool lines.

  ◆◆ Placing in local newspapers "letters to the editors" from the managers of Skil service centers that discussed the need to recycle batteries.

  ◆◆ Surveying hardware retailers on attitudes regarding environmentally friendly products and disseminating results to the media.

◆ Introduction of the products to media people at the annual National Hardware Show in a way they would never forget, a necessity since 1,000 exhibitors -- including power tool firms -- vie for media attention.

◆ Utilization of every other possible means to gain coverage, including ties to gift-buying holidays such as Christmas and Father's Day; photos of tools on magazine covers; ongoing one-on-one media contact; and inclusion in special sections such as *Associated Press'* home improvement and *Copley News Service*'s gift package.

CREATIVITY

The "creative centerpiece" of the campaign was how Flexi-Charge was introduced to media at the annual National Hardware Show.

Three weeks prior to the show, each editor received a wood box containing quality mixed nuts with a letter stating "the power snack" served as an invitation to the Skil exhibit to see the new, powerful Flexi-Charge line.

And, to emphasize the flexibility of the line, editors could schedule a "flexi-time" product briefing appointment at their convenience. At the booth, editors, like the Flexi-Charge tools, could easily "recharge their battery" by receiving a special "battery pack" (a large Skil-imprinted tote bag) filled with snacks.

Fifty-two scheduled personal meetings occurred, an effort that generated publicity results for the next 18 months. In fact, several media returned to the next year's Hardware Show carrying their Skil "recharging battery pack (totebag)."

The other tactics described above, such as the battery collection program, letters to the editors and poll of retailers, illustrated additional creative approaches that riveted attention on the Skil lines.

RESULTS

Extensive editorial coverage, and positioning the cordless tools as a dramatic cut above all others in the market, were achieved.

The positive awareness gained enabled Skil to exceed its sales targets by 25 percent.

The media themselves declared these tools as strikingly different and innovative. *Popular Science* named Flexi-Charge as one of the year's greatest achievements in science and technology. *Home Mechanix* selected the line as one of the best-value home improvement products of the year and prominently featured Flexi-Charge on a cover.

116

The cordless trim saw was dubbed a "small wonder" by *Workbench* magazine and described as "love at first cut" by *Popular Science*.

Other highlights:

- ◆ *NBC-TV*'s "The Today Show" and its "Gadget Guru" Andy Pargh provided coverage three times over the course of one year; Flexi-Charge was part of segments tied to Father's Day and the National Hardware Show, and the cordless circular saw was featured in a special innovative tools segment.

- ◆ Flexi-Charge and the results of the survey of retailers on environmental issues aired on the *CBS Radio Network* (some 240 stations), the Voice of America and the "Environmental Infoline" syndicated program airing on 273 stations, with a combined audience of more than 10 million.

- ◆ Flexi-Charge was described on the front page of *The Wall Street Journal*.

- ◆ *Associated Press, Reuters, King Features* (two times), *Copley News Service* and *Tribune Media Services* were among the news wires/syndicates describing the products, providing coverage in hundreds of newspapers.

- ◆ Major daily newspaper coverage was extensive, complemented by coverage generated through distribution of two newspaper mat releases, one tied to holiday gifts, the other to fall home improvement.

- ◆ *Rural Builder* magazine ran the cordless circular saw on its cover.

- Numerous stories on the battery collection program ran in newspapers and trade journals and many letters to the editors on the need to recycle (with a description of the new cordless tools) were published in major newspapers such as the *Milwaukee Journal, Portland Oregonian* and *St. Louis Post-Dispatch*.

- An important secondary market -- women -- was reached via coverage in publications such as *Better Homes & Gardens* and *Woman's Day*.

Case History

Taste of Chicago

OBJECTIVES

How does one surpass the past success of Chicago's largest, most popular festival, the Taste of Chicago (TOC)? In 1989, different challenges were issued by the new Richard M. Daley Administration to the Mayor's Office of Special Events.

In addition to meeting set goals in terms of attendance and food and beverage sales, the public relations team was charged with stressing the many family-oriented attractions to be offered at TOC, gaining attendance from more people residing outside the Chicago area to the eight-day extravaganza, and ensuring positive, upbeat press coverage, while redirecting possible media focus on alcohol sales and unruly crowds (such coverage had occurred in previous years).

After developing a theme -- "Eat To The Beat" -- that conveyed the essence of TOC (glorious food and never-ending musical entertainment), communications efforts were launched in late spring to inform Chicagoans, suburbanites, Midwesterners and the rest of the country that Chicago's lakefront was the place to be during TOC.

TECHNIQUES

A complete menu of public relations techniques helped meet objectives. The appetizer that whet the appetites of both media and the public was the TOC press preview, attended by more than 200

119

media people. In addition to sampling the culinary delights, the press was served up information from Mayor Daley and the special events director about the many new family attractions planned.

Other "courses" served prior to the opening included:

- A special mini-TOC held at LaRabida Hospital that helped promote the family theme, gained broadcast coverage and provided joy to youngsters who otherwise could not attend TOC.

- Placement of TOC press materials in the monthly mailing packet distributed to 1,000 travel writers by the Chicago Tourism Council to encourage family trips to Chicago and TOC.

- Arrangement to distribute TOC brochures by Amtrak and Metra rail services to reach business people and their families and to inform Midwest travelers.

- Development of special materials presented at meetings attended by TOC food vendors. The information provided guidelines on how vendors can assist in the public relations effort.

- Preparation of radio public service announcements that provided information on special public transportation schedules.

- Development of promotional announcements for use in advance of TOC by the eight radio stations broadcasting from Grant Park during the event.

- Arrangement for the special events director to discuss TOC during a Chicago Cubs telecast on superstation *WGN-TV*. The station also aired promotional announcements during the weekend prior to opening.

♦ Implementation of a comprehensive media relations effort that emphasized the family theme and reached out to media regionally and nationally, with a special effort to gain coverage on national television.

With the grand opening, the main course arrived. Activities included:

♦ Staging an opening parade led by Mayor Daley, followed by the children of TOC vendors, again to stress the family/children theme.

♦ Issuance of daily alerts to the media to help guide them toward positive TOC family and entertainment activities (such as appearances by Mickey Mouse, Sesame Street characters and homemaker Martha Stewart) in addition to providing daily figures on attendance and food consumption.

♦ Arrangement of special media stunts to herald the festival, ranging from the Chili Cook-off (sponsored, naturally, by Pepto-Bismol) to turning a *Chicago Sun-Times* reporter into a chocolate-covered correspondent.

♦ Delivery of special letters to all TV weathermen to encourage to mention TOC during forecasts.

♦ Delivery of mini-TOC food samplings to morning radio DJs to encourage discussion of the festival.

- Dishing up food consumption statistics covering the total TOC fun-filled feast.

Public relations representatives also staffed TOC daily from opening to close to coordinate interviews, respond to media inquiries, and direct media to cover the positive events and activities.

RESULTS

Judged solely by the numbers, TOC 1989 was a huge success. Record sales ($9.8 million) and attendance ($2.8 million) levels were reached, breaking the previous record-setting TOC even though 1989 was two days shorter.

But figures do not convey the complete story. TOC did draw more parents and children when compared to previous years, attested by comments from city staff and statistics, for example, that showed soda pop consumption was markedly up. Publicity was unsurpassed in terms of its scope. TOC was covered daily in Chicago's major newspapers and on TV news and radio stations; gained national television coverage on the syndicated program "Entertainment Tonight" and *Cable News Network*; and was covered extensively regionally in newspapers in cities such as Detroit, Des Moines, Cincinnati and Indianapolis.

And, coverage indeed was upbeat, positive and often focused on the family-oriented activities. Some examples:

- "Taste of Chicago isn't just for adults anymore." (*Chicago Sun-Times*).

- "This year, Taste organizers are making a concerted effort to draw more families." (*Chicago Tribune*).

122

♦   "The crowds this year were more friendly because of the family theme." (*Chicago Sun-Times*).

♦   "More family fun to TOC." (*Lerner Newspapers*).

♦   "A family affair at Taste." (*Chicago Defender*).

Perhaps the headline to the final wrap-up story in the *Chicago Tribune* summed up the public relations best: "Taste figures all add up to sweet success."

Case History

Williams Electronics, Inc.

OBJECTIVES

At one point in time, Williams Electronics, Inc. was regarded as the industry leader and innovator in the manufacture and sales of coin-operated pinball games and shuffle alleys. Following that period, however, Williams experienced an alarming slippage in esteem and sales, attributable to several factors: 1) An increase in the number of competitors, both in the U.S. and abroad; 2) Williams lagged a year behind other manufacturers, which had gained a marketing advantage by being first to utilize revolutionary solid state electronics technology to produce a new generation of exciting game features that proved appealing to players; and 3) Williams lacked a formal program to communicate effectively with its vital market base -- distributors who purchase the games and operators who place them in public locations.

Recognizing the need to reverse this downward trend, Williams initiated a revitalization. The Chicago-headquartered international company:

♦　　　Hired a new president with extensive background in the field of microprocessors and solid state electronics.

♦　　　Transformed its entire design and production operations to solid state electronics.

125

- Created games with new, fresh features such as memory banks, digital scoring and flashing light sequences coupled with multiple sounds.

- Communicated to its very select and influential market that a renaissance was indeed occurring at Williams.

The public relations objective was to communicate the following messages frequently and prominently to the distributor and operator audience: 1) Williams not only has transformed its entire operations to solid state electronics, but added game features that no other manufacturer has developed; 2) Due to these innovations, Williams games will produce more profits that games of its competitors; 3) The new technology is backed by quality products and components, and the company's servicing is prompt and efficient; and 4) Williams executives are authorities in solid state electronics technology and serve the industry as knowledgeable spokesmen and leaders.

TECHNIQUES

A publicity blitz was launched to reach this influential audience via the trade magazine "bibles": *RePlay, Play Meter, Cash Box* and *Vending Times* (and in Canada, *Canadian Coin Box*). Publicity techniques were divided into six categories:

- Profiles of Williams management positioned each as an authority in the industry by forecasting trends, offering opinions on recent developments and discussing the image of the industry.

- Feature articles broadened awareness of Williams and its advances by reporting on special meetings and events such as a product preview meeting for distributors, a pinball tournament and an exhibit

126

at the Amusement and Music Operators Association's (AMOA) convention.

- ♦ While consumer publicity was not a major goal, articles were developed in such media as the *Chicago Tribune, UPI*, and *ABC-TV* network news for the purpose of reporting the publicity back to distributors and operators through the trade media and reprints. This exhibited Williams' industry-leading position and its growing national reputation.

- ♦ Placement of game production photos that portrayed Williams' quality control reinforced the firm's pledge to distributors and operators of innovative products and games that are reliable.

- ♦ News stories on Williams' new testing equipment and service schools highlighted the firm's accelerated service program.

- ♦ New product stories and photos went beyond the routine industry release to explain in detail how game innovations produce increased profits for distributors and operators.

RESULTS

The program produced publicity results credited by Williams as unparalleled in the industry:

- ♦ A total of 99 stories were published in a 12-month period.

- ♦ Publicity attention to Williams "snowballed" to such an extent the firm selected "The Hot One" as its advertising theme halfway through the year.

♦ With the message that Williams' games were leading the industry in innovative features through broadened use of solid state electronics technology, the demand for the machines often exceeded the supply.

♦ Williams' "World Cup" game became its best seller in years, only to be exceeded a few months later by its "Disco Fever."

♦ Williams' image among the distributors and operators benefited remarkably. Both groups were quoted by trade media as acknowledging Williams' return as a vital force in the industry.

♦ The Williams exhibit at the AMOA convention drew the largest crowds.

♦ Competitors took note as well, many increasing their efforts in the promotional and publicity field by hiring outside agencies to combat Williams' efforts.

♦ Williams' president was selected as *Play Meter*'s "Coinman of the Month." The magazine credited his involvement "in a lot of public relations work for the industry... obviously, (he) places a great deal of importance in the image of this industry."

As expressed by the publication, this attitude, nonexistent only 12 months earlier among any representatives in the industry, typified the renewed confidence and interest in Williams' products. The remarkable transformation proved that a company's commitment to improve its products, image and communications can indeed turn a company's fortune quickly.